Trustworthiness

by Lucia Raatma

WITHDRAWN

CHERRY LAKE PUBLISHING * ANN ARBOR, MICHIGAN

Published in the United States of America by Cherry Lake Publishing
Ann Arbor, Michigan
www.cherrylakepublishing.com

Content Adviser: David Wangaard, Executive Director, SEE: The School for Ethical Education, Milford, Connecticut

Reading Adviser: Marla Conn, ReadAbility, Inc.

Photo Credits: Cover, ©Felix Mizioznikov/Shutterstock, Inc.; page 4, ©iStockphoto.com/erierika; page 6, ©Michal Kowalski/Shutterstock, Inc.; page 8, ©Jyn Meyer/Shutterstock, Inc.; page 10, ©karelnoppe/Shutterstock, Inc.; page 12, ©Petro Feketa/Dreamstime.com; page 14, ©iStockphoto.com/Blue_Cutler; page 16, ©Couperfield/Shutterstock, Inc.; page 18, ©Morgan Lane Photography/Shutterstock, Inc.; page 20, ©Monkey Business Images/Shutterstock, Inc.

LIBRARY OF CONGRESS CATALOGING-IN-PUBLICATION DATA
Raatma, Lucia.
  Trustworthiness/by Lucia Raatma.
      pages cm.—(Character education) (21st century junior library)
  Includes bibliographical references and index.
  ISBN 978-1-62431-159-8 (lib. bdg.)—ISBN 978-1-62431-225-0 (e-book)—
ISBN 978-1-62431-291-5 (pbk.)
  1. Trust—Juvenile literature. 2. Reliability—Juvenile literature. I. Title.
  BJ1500.T78R33 2013
  179'.9—dc23   2013004935

Cherry Lake Publishing would like to acknowledge the work of
The Partnership for 21st Century Skills.
Please visit www.p21.org for more information.

Printed in the United States of America
Corporate Graphics Inc.
July 2013
CLFA13

CONTENTS

Your teacher will appreciate your honesty
if you avoid copying someone else's work.

What Is Trustworthiness?

Sally saw her science teacher drop a paper. It was the answers to that day's test!

"Excuse me, Ms. White," she said. "You dropped this."

Ms. White smiled. She took the test answers from Sally. "Thanks," she said. "Not everyone is as trustworthy as you are."

Your family and friends will be understanding if
you admit your mistakes.

People can count on you when you are trustworthy. You do what you say you're going to do.

Melanie is a trustworthy person. She tells the truth. She **admits** her mistakes even when it might be easier to lie. You do the right thing when you are trustworthy.

Think!

What would the world be like if you couldn't trust anyone? What if even your parents and your best friend lied to you? Think of things that might happen if no one was trustworthy.

Your parents will trust you if you do your chores
the right way and get them done on time.

Being Trustworthy

There are many ways to be trustworthy at home. Steven is **reliable** when his parents ask him to do his chores. He finishes them as soon as he can. He does a good job. He does not just try to get it over with. That lets people know they can count on him to get things done.

Keeping promises to your friends is an important part of being trustworthy.

Being trustworthy means keeping your promises. This means doing what you say you'll do. A trustworthy person does not let other people down.

Miles promised to help his friend Betty work on a project after school. He showed that he was trustworthy by keeping his word. If you don't keep your word, your friends may not be able to count on you again.

If you are caught cheating, people will not trust you.

You can be trustworthy at school, too. Catherine is trustworthy. She never **cheats** on tests or homework. Sometimes it might be **tempting** to copy someone else's answers. That is never the right thing to do. Your classmates and teachers will not **respect** you if you cheat.

Create!

Make up a story about someone who isn't trustworthy. What might happen to the person? Would he or she learn a lesson about being trustworthy? Tell your story to a parent or a friend when it is done.

Stealing from other people breaks their trust in you.

You are trustworthy when you don't take things that belong to other people. Tyler's friend Jeremy has a new video game that he really wants to play. Jeremy left Tyler alone in his room one day when he was visiting. Did Tyler steal the game? No! A trustworthy person doesn't steal. People who are trustworthy earn money and save up for the things they want to buy.

Finding something on the ground does not mean
that it belongs to you.

Spreading Trust

The way you act **affects** other people. If you are trustworthy, other people might be, too. Danny was in a store. He saw someone drop money and walk away. The person didn't know she dropped it. Danny picked it up and gave it back to her. Your honesty may **inspire** other people to be honest, too.

Helping your family and neighbors with chores can help build their trust in you.

You can be trustworthy in your **community**. Do not take things from your neighbors or damage their property. Instead, lend a hand when they need help. Katie offered to do yard work when the family that lives next door was out of town. Make sure you keep your word if you promise to help.

Look!

Pay attention to the people you trust the most. What is it that makes them trustworthy? What can you do to be more like these people?

Trust will help you build strong relationships with your family and friends.

People know they can rely on you when you are trustworthy. You get along better with your family and friends. They know that you act in ways that are honest and fair. You will feel good knowing you have earned their trust!

Ask Questions!

Your parents might ask you to do a new chore. Make sure you understand what they want you to do. Ask questions to be sure you know what they expect. They will trust you if they know you are trying hard to do your best.

GLOSSARY

admits (ad-MITS) agrees that something is true; confesses to something

affects (uh-FEKTS) changes someone or something

cheats (CHEETS) acts dishonestly to get the right answer or win a game

community (kuh-MYOO-nuh-tee) a group of people who live in the same area or who have something in common with one another

inspire (in-SPIRE) to encourage or influence someone to do something

reliable (ri-LYE-uh-buhl) describing someone whom others can depend on and trust

respect (ri-SPEKT) to admire or have a high opinion of someone

tempting (TEMP-teeng) pleasing or appealing